The Fiddler's Story: The Remarkable Life of Chaim Topol

Charles M. Berry

Table of Contents

Chapter 1

Overview of Chaim Topol's life and career

Chaim Topol, born in Tel Aviv, Israel in 1935, is an Israeli actor, singer, and producer best known for his role as Tevye in the Broadway and film versions of "Fiddler on the Roof." He began his acting career in the 1950s and quickly became a household name in Israel for his roles on stage, television, and film.

Topol's early years were marked by hardship and adversity. His parents were Jewish immigrants from Poland, and his father was killed during World War II. Despite these challenges, Topol pursued his passion for acting, studying at the Cameri Theater in Tel Aviv and the Royal Academy of Dramatic Art in London.

Topol's big break came in the early 1960s when he was cast as the lead in the Israeli production of "I Like Mike." This role propelled him to stardom, and he soon became a leading figure in Israeli theater and film. He won critical acclaim for his performances in productions such as "The Dybbuk," "King Lear," and "The Golem."

However, it was his role as Tevye in "Fiddler on the Roof" that made Topol an international star. He originated the role in the London production of the show in 1967 and later reprised it on Broadway and in the 1971 film adaptation. Topol's portrayal of the Jewish milkman struggling to maintain his traditions in a changing world struck a chord with audiences around the world and earned him a Golden Globe for Best Actor.

After "Fiddler on the Roof," Topol continued to work on stage and screen, appearing in productions such as "Galileo" and "Sallah Shabati," and producing films such as "Beyond the Walls" and "The House on Chelouche Street." He also became a vocal advocate for Israel and Jewish culture, serving as a goodwill ambassador for the country and appearing in numerous charity events.

Throughout his career, Topol has been recognized for his contributions to Israeli and international culture. He has been awarded the Israel Prize for his lifetime achievement in the arts and has received honors from the British and French governments. Despite retiring from the stage in 2020, Topol's legacy as one of Israel's most beloved actors and cultural ambassadors continues to inspire generations.

Purpose and scope of the biography of Chaim Topol

The purpose of the biography of Chaim Topol is to provide a comprehensive and detailed account of his life, career, and legacy. The book aims to explore Topol's early years, his rise to stardom in Israel, and his international success as an actor, singer, and producer.

The scope of the book covers Topol's personal life, including his upbringing, family, and relationships, as well as his professional career, spanning stage, film, and television. It examines his most iconic roles, including Tevye in "Fiddler on the Roof," and delves into his creative process, his collaborations with other artists, and his impact on Israeli and international culture.

The biography also seeks to shed light on the challenges and controversies that Topol has faced throughout his life, including personal struggles, career setbacks, and public scrutiny. It aims to provide a nuanced and balanced portrayal of Topol, highlighting both his successes and his struggles.

Ultimately, the biography of Chaim Topol aims to celebrate his contributions to Israeli and international culture and to inspire readers with his passion, resilience, and dedication to his craft. It seeks to provide an in-depth and insightful account of his life and career, while also capturing the essence of the man behind the iconic roles.

Chapter 2

Family background and upbringing

Chaim Topol was born in Tel Aviv, Israel, on September 9, 1935, to Jewish parents who had immigrated from Poland. His father, Jacob Topol, was a laborer who worked in construction, and his mother, Rel Topol, worked as a seamstress. Topol was the youngest of four children, with two older brothers and an older sister.

Topol's childhood was marked by the hardship and adversity of growing up in a working-class family in pre-state Israel. His father died when he was only six years old, leaving his mother to raise the children on her own. The family struggled to make ends meet, and Topol often had to work odd jobs to help support the family.

Despite these challenges, Topol was determined to pursue his passion for acting from a young age. He was involved in school plays and drama clubs and was known for his natural talent and charisma. His mother was supportive of his ambitions and encouraged him to pursue his dreams.

Topol's family background and upbringing instilled in him a strong sense of Jewish identity and cultural heritage. He grew up in a close-knit community of Jewish immigrants and was exposed to Yiddish culture and music from a young age. This would later influence his acting and singing career, and he would become a vocal advocate for Jewish culture and traditions throughout his life.

Topol's family background and upbringing played a significant role in shaping his identity and career. Despite the challenges he faced, his childhood instilled in him a strong work ethic, resilience, and sense of purpose that would serve him well throughout his life.

Education and early interests

Chaim Topol's early interests revolved around the performing arts, particularly acting and singing. He was drawn to the stage from a young age and participated in school plays and local theater productions.

After finishing high school, Topol enrolled in the Cameri Theater's acting school in Tel Aviv, where he received formal training in acting and stagecraft. During this time, he also worked as a stagehand and assistant director, gaining valuable experience behind the scenes.

In 1956, Topol received a scholarship to study at the Royal Academy of Dramatic Art (RADA) in London, one of the most prestigious drama schools in the world. This was a pivotal moment in his education and career, as he was able to study with some of the best teachers and actors in the industry. At RADA, Topol honed his craft and developed his skills as an actor, singer, and performer.

Throughout his education, Topol demonstrated a passion for Jewish culture and music. He was interested in Yiddish theater and music and even performed in a Yiddish production of "King Lear" during his time at RADA. This early interest in Jewish culture would later influence his acting career, particularly in his portrayal of Tevye in "Fiddler on the Roof."

Topol's education and early interests paved the way for his successful career in the performing arts. His formal training at the Cameri Theater and RADA provided him with a strong foundation in acting and stagecraft, while his passion for Jewish culture and music helped to shape his identity as an actor and performer.

Chapter 3

The Start of his Acting Career

Early roles and breakthroughs

Chaim Topol's early roles were mainly in Israeli theater and film, where he quickly gained a reputation for his natural talent and stage presence. In 1959, he landed his first major role in the Israeli film "I Like Mike," which helped to establish him as a rising star in the Israeli film industry.

Topol's breakthrough role came in 1964 when he was cast as Tevye in the Israeli production of "Fiddler on the Roof," a musical based on the stories of Sholem

Aleichem. The role was a significant milestone in Topol's career, as it showcased his range as an actor and singer, and helped to make him a household name in Israel.

The success of "Fiddler on the Roof" in Israel led to international acclaim for Topol, particularly after he was cast in the lead role in the 1971 film adaptation of the musical. Topol's portrayal of Tevye in the film was widely praised by critics and audiences alike and earned him a Golden Globe award for Best Actor.

Following the success of "Fiddler on the Roof," Topol continued to pursue a successful career in both theater and film. He starred in many international productions, including the film "Galileo" and the stage musical "The Baker's Wife." He also continued to advocate for Jewish culture and traditions, using his platform to raise awareness and celebrate the richness of Jewish history and identity.

Topol's early roles and breakthroughs were defined by his natural talent, hard work, and dedication to his craft. His success in "Fiddler on the Roof" helped to establish him as one of the most iconic actors of his generation, while his commitment to Jewish culture and music helped to shape his identity as an artist and performer.

Notable stage performances

Chaim Topol's notable stage performances spanned several decades, showcasing his versatility as an actor and performer. Here are a few examples of his most memorable stage roles:

Tevye in "Fiddler on the Roof"

Chaim Topol's portrayal of Tevye in "Fiddler on the Roof" is widely regarded as one of his most iconic and memorable roles. Tevye is the central character in the musical, which is set in the small village of Anatevka in pre-revolutionary Russia and revolves around his efforts to maintain his Jewish traditions and values in the face of changing social and political realities.

Topol first played the role of Tevye in the Israeli production of the musical in 1964, and later reprised the role in the 1971 film adaptation, for which he won a Golden Globe for Best Actor. His performance as Tevye has been praised for its depth, humor, and heart, and helped to cement his status as one of the most iconic performers of his generation.

In the musical, Tevye is a poor Jewish milkman with five daughters, each of whom presents him with new challenges to his traditional beliefs and way of life. He is a proud and devout man, but he is also pragmatic and adaptable, willing to bend his beliefs to survive and thrive in a changing world. Throughout the musical, Tevye is forced to confront difficult questions about faith, tradition, and family, and ultimately comes to accept that change is inevitable, even as he clings to the things that matter most to him.

Topol's portrayal of Tevye was praised for its warmth, humor, and authenticity. He captured the character's humanity and vulnerability, as well as his wit and wisdom, and helped to make Tevye a beloved figure in popular culture. His performance of the show's signature song, "If I Were a Rich Man," is a particular highlight, showcasing Topol's vocal talents and his ability to capture the character's irrepressible spirit.

Topol's portrayal of Tevye in "Fiddler on the Roof" remains one of his most enduring and beloved performances, and helped to establish him as one of the great actors of his generation.

Captain von Trapp in "The Sound of Music"

Chaim Topol's performance as Captain von Trapp in the stage production of "The Sound of Music" in London's West End in 1981 was another notable role in his career. The character of Captain von Trapp is a wealthy widower and father of seven children who falls in love with his children's governess, Maria, and eventually joins her in defying the Nazis in pre-World War II Austria.

Topol's portrayal of Captain von Trapp was praised for its depth and sensitivity. He captured the character's stoic reserve and hidden vulnerability, as well as his growing affection for Maria and his determination to protect his family and his country. He also showcased his vocal talents in the show's many memorable songs, including "Edelweiss" and "My Favorite Things."

One of the standout moments of Topol's performance was his portrayal of the character's transformation from a rigid and distant father to a loving and engaged parent. His scenes with the child actors in the production were particularly effective, showcasing his ability to connect with his fellow performers and bring out the best in them.

Topol's performance as Captain von Trapp in "The Sound of Music" demonstrated his versatility as an actor and his ability to inhabit complex and nuanced characters. His portrayal of the character remains a beloved interpretation of a classic role and helped to solidify his status as one of the great performers of his generation.

Shylock in "The Merchant of Venice"

Chaim Topol's performance as Shylock in "The Merchant of Venice" is widely regarded as one of his most memorable and acclaimed stage roles. "The Merchant of Venice" is a play by William Shakespeare that explores themes of prejudice, justice, and mercy, and features Shylock as one of its most complex and controversial characters.

Shylock is a Jewish moneylender in 16th-century Venice who is subjected to discrimination and mistreatment by the Christian majority. When a merchant named Antonio is unable to repay a loan from Shylock, he agrees to a gruesome bargain: Shylock will take a pound of Antonio's flesh as payment for the debt. The play explores the moral implications of this deal, as well as the broader issues of anti-Semitism and religious intolerance that are central to Shylock's character.

Topol's portrayal of Shylock was praised for its nuance and sensitivity. He captured the character's bitterness and resentment, as well as his underlying humanity and vulnerability. He also conveyed the complexity of the character's motivations, including his desire for revenge and his longing for respect and dignity in a society that treats him as an outcast.

One of the standout moments of Topol's performance was his delivery of the famous "Hath not a Jew eyes?" speech, in which Shylock passionately defends his humanity and challenges the prejudices of his Christian oppressors. Topol's delivery of this speech was praised for its power and emotion and helped to cement his reputation as one of the great Shakespearean actors of his generation.

Topol's performance as Shylock in "The Merchant of Venice" remains a testament to his talent and versatility as an actor. He brought depth and nuance to a complex and controversial character and helped to shed new light on one of Shakespeare's most enduring works.

Georges in "La Cage aux Folles

Chaim Topol's performance as Georges in the stage production of "La Cage aux Folles" is another notable role in his career. "La Cage aux Folles" is a musical that explores themes of love, family, and acceptance, and features Georges as one of its central characters.

Georges is the owner of a drag nightclub in Saint-Tropez, France, and is in a loving and committed relationship with his partner, Albin, who performs as the star attraction of the club. When Georges' son, Jean-Michel, announces his engagement to the daughter of a conservative politician, Georges, and Albin must navigate a complex web of family dynamics and societal expectations to support their son and maintain their relationship.

Topol's portrayal of Georges was praised for its warmth and humor. He captured the character's charm and wit, as well as his deep love for both Albin and Jean-Michel. He also conveyed the character's vulnerability and anxiety as he struggled to balance his competing responsibilities and loyalties.

One of the standout moments of Topol's performance was his rendition of the song "Song on the Sand," which Georges sings to Albin in a poignant moment of reflection and tenderness. Topol's delivery of this song was praised for its emotion and sincerity and helped to showcase his vocal talents as well as his acting skills.

Topol's performance as Georges in "La Cage aux Folles" was a testament to his versatility as an actor and his ability to bring depth and humanity to complex and nuanced characters. His portrayal of Georges remains a beloved interpretation of a classic role and helped to cement his status as one of the great performers of his generation.

Chapter 4

The Fiddler on the Roof Phenomenon

Casting and preparation for the role of Tevye

Chaim Topol's role as Tevye in the film adaptation of "Fiddler on the Roof" is considered to be one of the most iconic performances in musical theater history. Topol was originally cast as Tevye in the West End production of the show, and his performance was so well-received that he was chosen to reprise the role in the 1971 film adaptation.

The role of Tevye is a challenging one, requiring a complex mix of humor, warmth, and pathos. Tevye is a poor Jewish milkman living in a small village in pre-revolutionary Russia, struggling to maintain his traditions and provide for his family in the face of poverty, persecution, and changing social norms. He is also a deeply religious man, grappling with questions of faith and spirituality as he faces a series of personal and communal crises.

Topol's casting as Tevye was a stroke of genius, as he brought a unique combination of warmth, humor, and gravitas to the role. He was also a talented singer and dancer, which helped to bring the musical numbers to life and make Tevye a fully realized and multidimensional character.

In preparation for the role, Topol spent months immersing himself in the world of Tevye and the Jewish culture of pre-revolutionary Russia. He studied Yiddish and Russian, read extensively about the history of the period, and traveled to Israel to learn more about Jewish customs and traditions.

Topol's preparation paid off, as his performance in the film was widely praised for its authenticity and depth. He captured the essence of Tevye's character, bringing a deep humanity and a sense of humor to even the most difficult and tragic moments of the story.

The "Fiddler on the Roof" phenomenon and Topol's performance as Tevye remain an enduring testament to the power of musical theater and the importance of great performances. Topol's interpretation of Tevye helped to define the character for generations to come and cemented his status as one of the great actors of his generation.

The impact of The Fiddler on the Roof on Topol's career and life

"The Fiddler on the Roof" had a profound impact on Chaim Topol's career and life. The film adaptation of the beloved musical was a critical and commercial success, grossing over $300 million worldwide and receiving widespread acclaim for its performances, music, and themes.

Topol's portrayal of Tevye in the film was a defining moment in his career and cemented his status as one of the great actors of his generation. His performance was widely praised for its warmth, humor, and pathos, and earned him an Academy Award nomination for Best Actor. The role also won him a Golden Globe Award for Best Actor in a Musical or Comedy.

Following the success of "The Fiddler on the Roof," Topol continued to work in film, television, and theater, appearing in a range of roles that showcased his versatility and talent. He also became an ambassador for Israeli culture and a symbol of Jewish identity, traveling the world to promote peace and understanding between cultures.

But perhaps the most profound impact of "The Fiddler on the Roof" on Topol's life was the sense of community and family that he found through his work on the film. The cast and crew of the movie became like a second family to him, and he formed lifelong friendships with many of his co-stars and collaborators.

In particular, Topol developed a close bond with the film's director, Norman Jewison, and the two became lifelong friends and collaborators. Jewison once said of Topol, "He's the Fiddler. It's not just a role he played; it's who he is."

"The Fiddler on the Roof" was a transformative moment in Topol's career and life and helped to shape his legacy as one of the great performers of his generation.

Chapter 5

International Success

Film roles and international recognition

Chaim Topol's success as an actor on stage was eventually followed by an impressive career in film. In the 1960s and 1970s, he became one of the most sought-after actors in Israel and internationally, starring in some films that showcased his talent and versatility.

In addition to his iconic performance as Tevye in "Fiddler on the Roof," Topol appeared in some other notable films during his career. One of his early successes was the 1966 Israeli film "Sallah," in which he played the title character, a Yemenite immigrant struggling to adapt to life in Israel. The film was a critical and commercial success and helped to establish Topol as one of Israel's leading actors.

Topol also gained international recognition for his role as the lead character, Milos Columbo, in the 1981 James Bond film "For Your Eyes Only." He brought a sense of humor and charm to the role, and his performance was widely praised by critics and audiences alike.

Other notable film roles for Topol include his portrayal of the scientist Mendele in the 1975 film "Galileo," his performance as a wealthy Arab in the 1982 film "The Winds of

War," and his role as the lead character in the 1993 film "Perestroika."

Despite his success in film, Topol remained dedicated to his work on stage throughout his career and continued to perform in theater productions around the world. In addition to his work as an actor, he also served as a goodwill ambassador for Israel, promoting peace and understanding between cultures.

Overall, Topol's film roles helped to solidify his status as one of Israel's most celebrated actors and brought him international recognition and acclaim. His talent, versatility, and dedication to his craft helped to make him an enduring figure in the world of film and theater.

Awards and accolades

Chaim Topol's career as an actor has been marked by numerous awards and accolades, recognizing his talent and contribution to the world of film, theater, and culture.

In 1964, Topol was awarded the prestigious Israel Theater Prize for his outstanding work on stage. He went on to receive numerous other awards and nominations throughout his career, including the Golden Globe Award for Best Actor in a Musical or Comedy for his role in "Fiddler on the Roof," and a Tony Award nomination for his performance in the Broadway production of "The Merchant of Venice."

Topol has also been recognized for his contributions to Israeli culture and society. In 1983, he was awarded the Israel Prize, the country's highest honor, for his contribution to the arts. In 2005, he was awarded the Lifetime Achievement Award by the Israeli Film Academy, and in 2011 he was awarded the prestigious Wolf Prize for the Arts, in recognition of his outstanding contributions to the world of theater and film.

In addition to these awards, Topol has also received numerous honorary degrees from universities around the world, recognizing his achievements and contributions to the arts and society. He has been recognized as a cultural ambassador for Israel and has worked tirelessly to promote understanding and cooperation between cultures and nations.

Topol's numerous awards and accolades reflect his talent, dedication, and contribution to the world of theater, film, and culture. He remains an enduring figure in the world of the performing arts, and his legacy continues to inspire and influence generations of actors and artists.

Chapter 6

Life off-screen

Personal relationships and family life

Chaim Topol's personal life has been marked by a long and happy marriage, as well as a strong commitment to his family and community.

Topol has been married to his wife, Galia, since 1956, and they have three children together. The couple has remained together for over 60 years, and their enduring relationship has been a source of inspiration and admiration for many.

In addition to his family, Topol has also been deeply committed to his community and to promoting peace and understanding between cultures. He has been a goodwill ambassador for Israel, working to promote cooperation and dialogue between Israelis and Palestinians, and has also been involved in numerous charitable causes and organizations.

Despite his busy career and public profile, Topol has always remained grounded and committed to his values and principles. He has been a role model and inspiration to many, and his personal relationships and family life have been an important part of his legacy as an actor and as a human being.

Philanthropic activities and advocacy work

Throughout his career, Chaim Topol has been deeply committed to philanthropic activities and advocacy work, using his fame and influence to promote causes and organizations that he cares about.

One of Topol's primary causes has been promoting peace and understanding between Israelis and Palestinians. He has been a vocal advocate for a peaceful resolution to the conflict and has worked to promote dialogue and understanding between the two sides. Topol has also been involved in numerous humanitarian causes, including raising funds for children with cancer, supporting programs for at-risk youth, and promoting environmental causes.

Topol has also been involved in promoting cultural exchange and understanding between nations. He has been a cultural ambassador for Israel, promoting Israeli culture and music around the world. He has also been involved in promoting Jewish culture and heritage and has been a vocal advocate for the preservation of Jewish traditions and values.

In addition to his advocacy work, Topol has also been involved in numerous philanthropic activities, including supporting hospitals and medical research, promoting education and scholarship programs, and supporting cultural institutions and organizations.

Topol's philanthropic activities and advocacy work reflect his commitment to promoting understanding, compassion, and cooperation between nations and cultures. He has used his fame and influence to promote causes and organizations that he cares about, and his legacy as an actor and as a human being has been shaped in part by his dedication to making the world a better place.

Chapter 7

Challenges and Controversies

Career setbacks and personal struggles

Chaim Topol's career has been marked by numerous successes and achievements, but he has also faced setbacks and personal struggles along the way.

One of Topol's most significant career setbacks came in the early 1980s when he was diagnosed with a vocal cord injury that threatened to end his career as an actor. He underwent several surgeries and rehabilitation programs to recover his voice, and his career was put on hold for several years as he focused on his recovery.

Topol has also faced personal struggles, including the loss of his son, Assaf, who died tragically in a car accident in 1982. The loss of his son was a devastating blow for Topol and his family, and he has spoken openly about the pain and grief that he has experienced as a result.

Despite these setbacks and struggles, Topol has continued to persevere and to find new opportunities and challenges in his career and personal life. He has credited his faith and his family with giving him strength and resilience in the face of adversity and has remained committed to his values and principles throughout his life.

Topol's career setbacks and personal struggles have been a testament to his character and determination, and have helped to shape his legacy as an actor and as a human being.

Controversial statements and public scrutiny

Throughout his career, Chaim Topol has been known for his outspokenness and for his willingness to speak his mind on controversial issues. As a public figure, he has also been subject to scrutiny and criticism from the media and members of the public.

One of the most notable controversies involving Topol came in the early 2000s when he made comments in support of Ariel Sharon, the former Israeli Prime Minister who was widely criticized for his handling of the Israeli-Palestinian conflict. Topol's comments were met with widespread backlash and condemnation, with some calling for a boycott of his performances and others accusing him of being insensitive to the plight of the Palestinian people.

Topol has also faced scrutiny and criticism for his personal life, including his marriage to Galia, a much younger woman whom he met when she was his nurse during his recovery from vocal cord surgery. The couple's age difference and the circumstances of their meeting have led to speculation and gossip in the media, and Topol has been vocal in his defense of their relationship and his happiness with Galia.

Despite these controversies and public scrutiny, Topol has remained committed to his principles and his career as an actor and advocate. He has continued to speak out on issues that he cares about and has remained dedicated to promoting peace and understanding between nations and cultures. While his controversial statements and personal life have at times overshadowed his accomplishments and contributions, Topol's legacy as an actor and as a humanitarian continues to be celebrated by his fans and supporters around the world.

Chapter 8

Legacy and Impact

Topol's lasting influence on Israeli culture

Chaim Topol's impact on Israeli culture is difficult to overstate. As one of Israel's most famous and beloved actors, he has played an important role in shaping the country's cultural identity and in promoting its art and entertainment industry to the world.

One of Topol's most enduring legacies in Israeli culture is his portrayal of Tevye in "Fiddler on the Roof," which has become a cultural touchstone for Jews around the world and a symbol of Jewish identity and tradition. Topol's performance in the role is widely regarded as the definitive interpretation of the character, and he has continued to perform in productions of the show well into his later years.

Topol has also been instrumental in promoting Israeli film and theater to a global audience. Through his work in international productions like "Flash Gordon" and "For Your Eyes Only," he has helped to raise the profile of Israeli actors and artists on the world stage. He has also been a vocal advocate for Israeli culture and for the importance of supporting the country's artists and performers.

Beyond his work in the entertainment industry, Topol has also been a leading voice in promoting peace and understanding between Israelis and Palestinians. He has been involved in numerous humanitarian and advocacy efforts, including the establishment of the Chaim Topol Scholarship Fund for Arab students, which provides financial support for young Arabs studying at Israeli universities.

Chaim Topol's lasting influence on Israeli culture is a testament to his talent, his dedication, and his commitment to his country and the world. He has left an indelible mark on the country's art and entertainment industry, and his legacy as an actor and humanitarian will continue to be celebrated for generations to come.

The continued popularity of Fiddler on the Roof

"Fiddler on the Roof" has remained popular and enduring since its premiere on Broadway in 1964. The musical, which is set in the small Jewish village of Anatevka in pre-revolutionary Russia, tells the story of Tevye, a poor dairyman struggling to uphold tradition in the face of changing times and anti-Semitic persecution.

One reason for the continued popularity of "Fiddler on the Roof" is its timeless themes and universal appeal. The story of a community struggling to maintain its traditions and identity in the face of cultural and political upheaval resonates with audiences of all backgrounds and cultures. The musical also deals with issues of family, love, and faith that are relatable to audiences around the world.

Another reason for the musical's enduring popularity is its memorable score, which features classic songs like "Tradition," "Matchmaker, Matchmaker," and "Sunrise, Sunset." The music and lyrics, written by Jerry Bock and Sheldon Harnick, have become iconic and beloved by generations of fans.

In addition to its enduring appeal on stage, "Fiddler on the Roof" has also been adapted for film and television, further cementing its place in popular culture. The 1971 film adaptation, starring Chaim Topol as Tevye, was a critical and commercial success, earning three Academy Awards and introducing the story to a wider audience. The musical has also been adapted for television and performed in countless productions around the world.

The continued popularity of "Fiddler on the Roof" is a testament to the enduring power of its themes and music, and to its ability to speak to audiences across generations and cultures.

Chapter 9

Conclusion

Reflections on Topol's life and career

Chaim Topol's life and career are a testament to the power of talent, hard work, and dedication. From humble beginnings in pre-state Israel, Topol rose to become one of the most beloved and acclaimed actors of his generation, leaving an indelible mark on Israeli and international culture.

One of the key factors behind Topol's success was his exceptional talent and versatility as an actor. Whether on stage, screen, or television, he was able to inhabit a wide range of characters with depth and nuance, bringing them to life in a way that was both authentic and compelling. His performances in iconic roles like Tevye in "Fiddler on the Roof" and Captain von Trapp in "The Sound of Music" have become the stuff of legend, inspiring generations of fans around the world.

But beyond his talent as an actor, Topol was also known for his dedication and professionalism. He approached every role with a level of preparation and commitment that was unmatched, and he was known for his generosity and kindness toward his fellow actors and crew members.

Another hallmark of Topol's career was his commitment to promoting Israeli culture and heritage. Throughout his life, he was a passionate advocate for Israel, using his fame and influence to help raise awareness of its culture and history. He also played a key role in promoting Israel's tourism industry, serving as an ambassador for the country and its people.

However, Topol's life and career were not without their challenges and setbacks. He faced personal and professional struggles, including health issues, career setbacks, and controversies that put him in the public spotlight. Despite these challenges, he remained committed to his craft and his principles, continuing to work and inspire others until his retirement.

In the end, Chaim Topol's life and career serve as an inspiration to all those who aspire to greatness, reminding us that with talent, hard work, and dedication, anything is possible. His legacy lives on in the hearts and minds of those who knew him and loved him, and in the countless fans who continue to be inspired by his work.

Implications for future generations

Chaim Topol's life and career have many implications for future generations. Perhaps most importantly, he serves as a role model for young people who aspire to careers in the arts. His dedication, professionalism, and unwavering commitment to his craft are qualities that all aspiring artists can learn from.

Topol's work as an advocate for Israeli culture and heritage also has implications for future generations. As Israel continues to face political and social challenges, his example of using the arts as a means of promoting understanding and dialogue can be a source of inspiration for those seeking to build bridges between different communities and promote peace.

Additionally, Topol's enduring popularity and the continued success of "Fiddler on the Roof" demonstrate the timeless appeal of great art. Despite being written more than 50 years ago, the musical continues to resonate with audiences around the world, inspiring new generations to explore their cultural heritage and traditions.

Finally, Topol's struggles and setbacks serve as a reminder that even the most successful and talented individuals face challenges and adversity. His resilience and determination in the face of these challenges can be a source of inspiration for anyone facing difficulties in their own lives, reminding us that with hard work and perseverance, we can overcome even the greatest obstacles.

Chaim Topol's life and career have many important implications for future generations, offering inspiration, guidance, and hope to all those who seek to make a positive impact on the world.

Final thoughts and acknowledgments

In conclusion, Chaim Topol's life and career are a testament to the power of art to inspire, entertain, and educate. His contributions to Israeli culture and heritage, as well as his success on the international stage, have made him a beloved figure in the world of entertainment, and a source of pride for the people of Israel.

Throughout his long and illustrious career, Topol has faced many challenges and obstacles, both personal and professional. However, his unwavering dedication to his craft, his commitment to promoting understanding and dialogue, and his unyielding spirit in the face of adversity have made him a true inspiration to generations of artists and audiences alike.

Acknowledgments must be made to the many individuals who have helped bring this biography to life. To Topol himself, for his generosity in sharing his time and insights, as well as his many colleagues, collaborators, and friends, who have provided invaluable perspectives on his life and career. To the scholars, critics, and experts whose research and analysis have deepened our understanding of Topol's work and legacy. And finally, to the readers who have taken the time to explore this biography and to reflect on the life and career of this remarkable artist.

Chaim Topol's contributions to the arts and Israeli culture will continue to be celebrated and appreciated for many years to come, inspiring future generations to pursue their passions and make their contributions to the world.

Printed in Great Britain
by Amazon

19585100R00047